MRJC

Geology Zone

Ores

by Julie Murray

Dash!
LEVELED READERS
An Imprint of Abdo Zoom • abdobooks.com

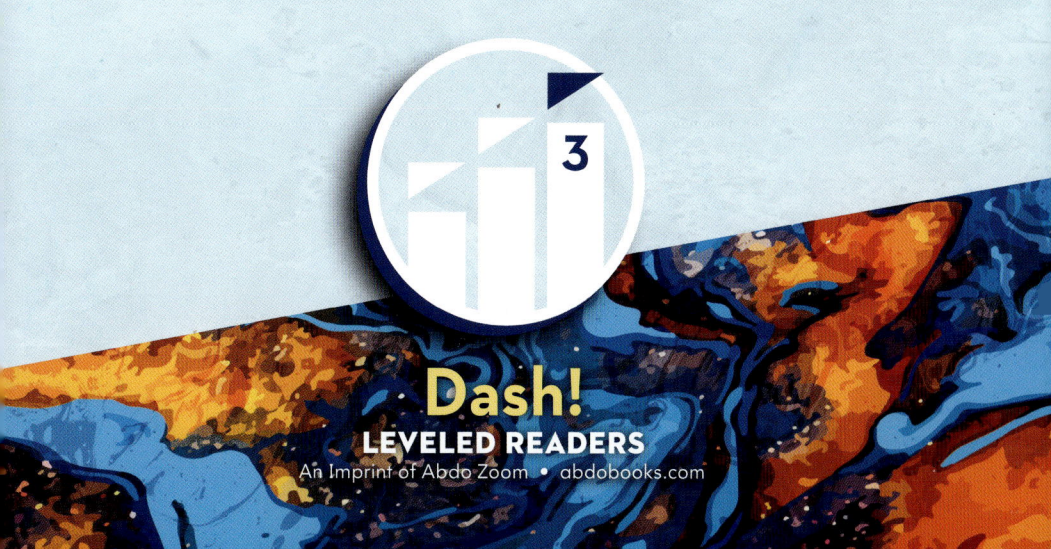

Level 1 – Beginning
Short and simple sentences with familiar words or patterns for children who are beginning to understand how letters and sounds go together.

Level 2 – Emerging
Longer words and sentences with more complex language patterns for readers who are practicing common words and letter sounds.

Level 3 – Transitional
More developed language and vocabulary for readers who are becoming more independent.

THIS BOOK CONTAINS RECYCLED MATERIALS

abdobooks.com

Published by Abdo Zoom, a division of ABDO, PO Box 398166, Minneapolis, Minnesota 55439. Copyright © 2025 by Abdo Consulting Group, Inc. International copyrights reserved in all countries. No part of this book may be reproduced in any form without written permission from the publisher. Dash!™ is a trademark and logo of Abdo Zoom.

Printed in the United States of America, North Mankato, Minnesota.
102024
012025

Photo Credits: Getty Images, Shutterstock
Production Contributors: Kenny Abdo, Jennie Forsberg, Grace Hansen, John Hansen
Design Contributors: Candice Keimig, Neil Klinepier

Library of Congress Control Number: 2024936541

Publisher's Cataloging in Publication Data
Names: Murray, Julie, author.
Title: Ores / by Julie Murray
Description: Minneapolis, Minnesota : Abdo Zoom, 2025 | Series: Geology zone | Includes online resources and index.
Identifiers: ISBN 9781098287184 (lib. bdg.) | ISBN 9781098287887 (ebook) | ISBN 9781098288235 (Read-to-me ebook)
Subjects: LCSH: Ores--Juvenile literature. | Ore deposits--Juvenile literature. | Rocks--Identification--Juvenile literature. | Geology--Juvenile literature. | Earth sciences--Juvenile literature.
Classification: DDC 553.8--dc23

Table of Contents

Ores 4

Mining Ores 12

Metals from Ores 18

More Facts 22

Glossary 23

Index 24

Online Resources 24

Ores

Ores are naturally occurring rocks that are found in Earth's **crust**. Ores contain **minerals** such as gold, iron, or lead.

Ores form in different ways. Some form from cooling magma. When magma is trapped under Earth's surface, it cools slowly. This causes large **mineral** grains to form.

When magma reaches the surface, it is called lava. Lava quickly cools and hardens. This forms large rocks that contain **minerals** too.

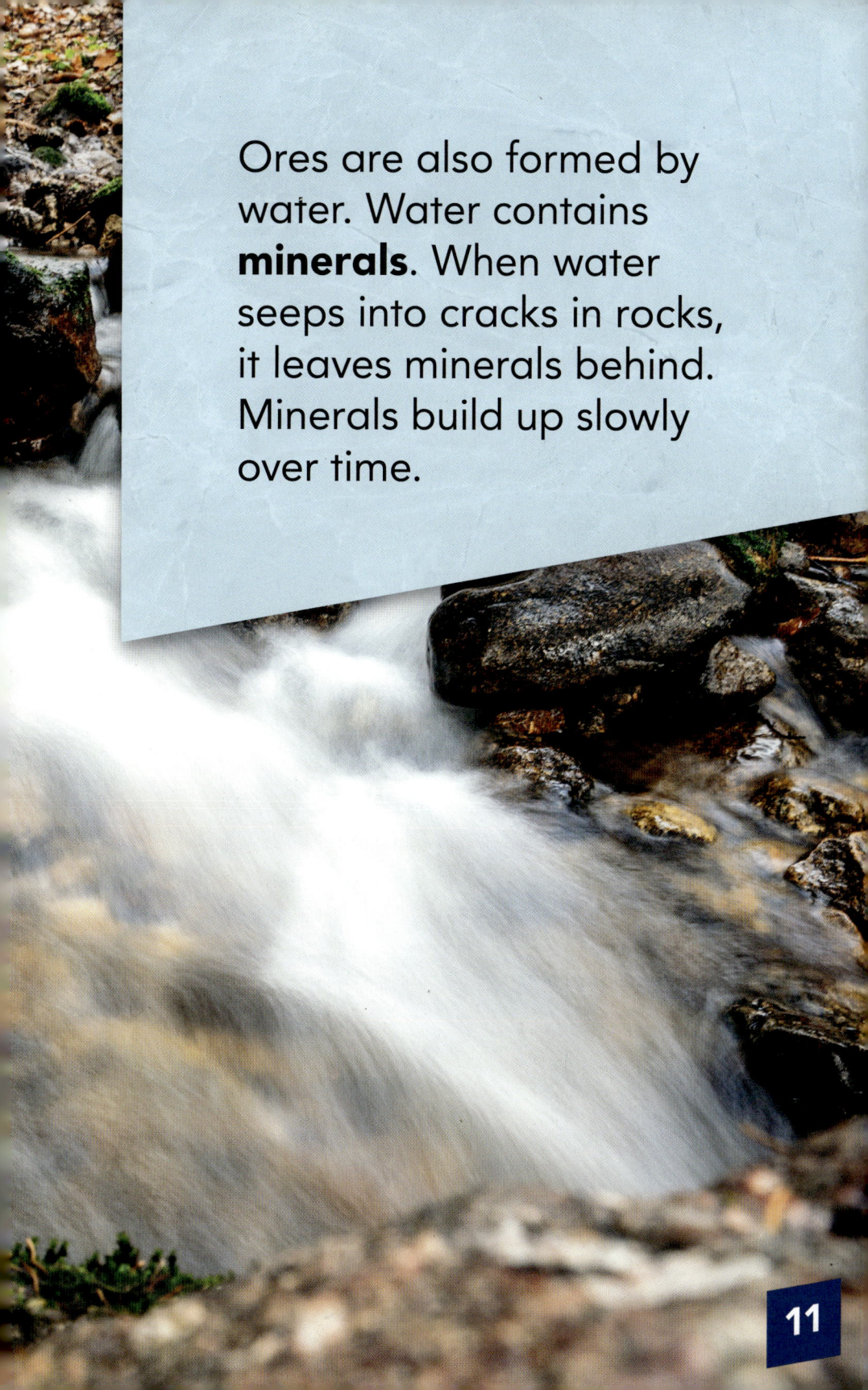

Ores are also formed by water. Water contains **minerals**. When water seeps into cracks in rocks, it leaves minerals behind. Minerals build up slowly over time.

Mining Ores

Humans **mine** ore to take out and use the valuable **minerals** and other materials. First, rocks containing ore must be dug out of the ground. This is a big job!

The rocks are then crushed by large machines. Next, the **minerals** are extracted from the rocks. This is done by **smelting** or electrolysis.

Ore can also be found deep in the Earth. Miners go into deep tunnels to reach ore deposits. In underground mining, the rock needs to be blasted.

Metals from Ores

Copper, iron, and gold are all metal ores that are **mined**. They are used to make everyday items. Copper, for example, is used in electrical wiring.

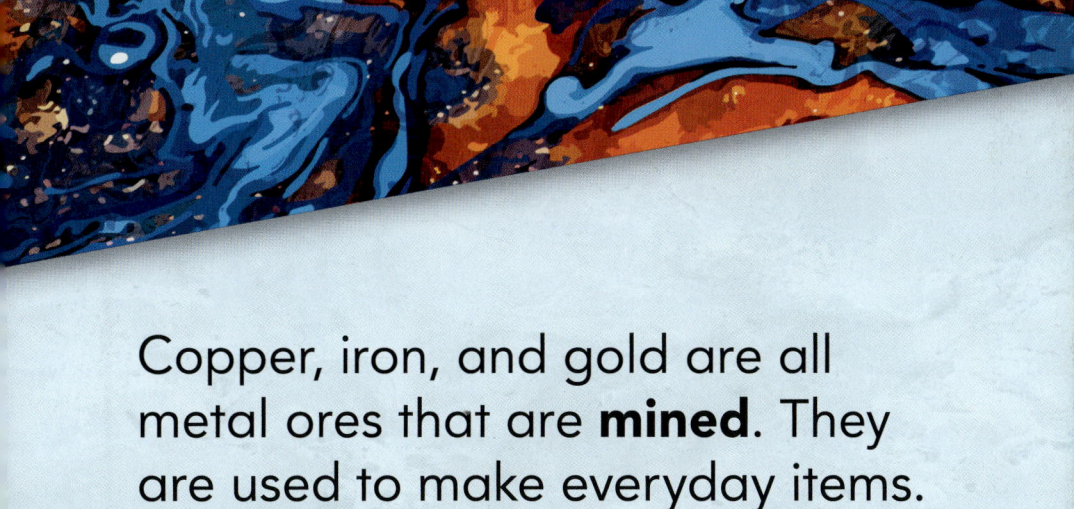

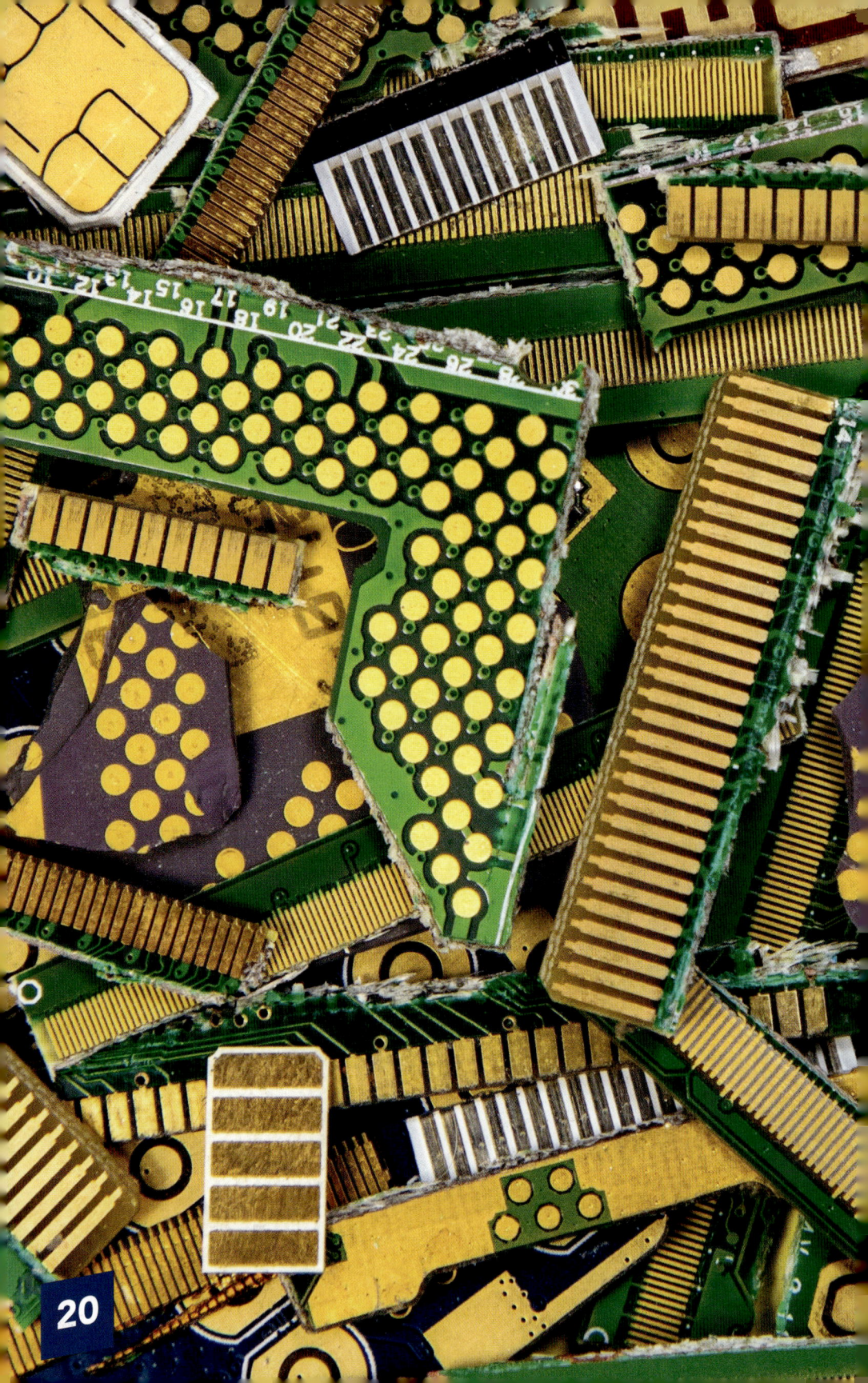

Iron is a strong metal. It is used to make machine parts and other products. Gold is a **precious metal**. It is used in electronics and to make jewelry.

More Facts

- Ore deposits are found all around the world. Lead, copper, and iron are all common metals that are obtained from ore in the United States.

- Some types of ore can take millions of years to form.

- More than 6,613,868 pounds (3,000,000 kg) of gold is mined in the world each year!

Glossary

crust – the outer layer of Earth.

mine – to dig out from the earth.

mineral – a substance formed in the earth that is not of an animal or a plant.

precious metal – a rare, naturally occurring metallic chemical element of high economic value.

smelting – melting or fusing in order to separate and obtain the metal content.

Index

electrical wiring 19

electronics 21

formation 6, 9, 11

jewelry 21

machine parts 21

magma 6, 9

metal 5, 19, 21

minerals 5

mining 12, 16

water 11

Online Resources

Booklinks
NONFICTION NETWORK
FREE! ONLINE NONFICTION RESOURCES

To learn more about ores, please visit **abdobooklinks.com** or scan this QR code. These links are routinely monitored and updated to provide the most current information available.